MARKS &
SPENCER

My
HORSE &
PONY
Book

Written by Gaby Goldsack
Photography by Martin Haswell

Marks and Spencer p.l.c.
PO Box 3339
Chester CH99 9QS
www.marksandspencer.com

ISBN 1-84461-398-4

Printed in China

Equestrian consultant: Karen Griggs
Photoshoot consultant: Chris Scollen

Acknowledgements
The publisher would also like to thank the following for their help in the production of this book:

Stonar School, Wiltshire, for their kind permission to photograph this book at their equestrian centre, with special thanks to the centre's director Jill Storey and all her staff; our young riders Fay A'Bear, Jonty Bevins, Beau Carrel, Yolanda Edwards, Katherine Lambert, Libby Seed and Henry Stafford-Charles; farrier Mike Roberts; horse-handler Valerie Allen; Wadswick Country Stores, Wiltshire, for the loan and hire of equipment; Widbrook Equestrian Centre, Wiltshire, for allowing us to shoot some of the pictures on their premises.
Please note that the names on the following pages have been changed to protect the children's identity.

Cover Photo: Thea Lawson and her pony Pepsi (Peter Lawson)

Additional photography supplied by: Horsepix (page 6 top left, page 7 middle left, pages 8-9 middle left, page 9 top right/bottom right, page 57 top/bottom, page 60 bottom); Bob Langrish (page 8 top left/bottom left, page 60 top left/middle left); Peter Lawson (page 54 top left, page 53 bottom right, page 59 top); Soley Photos (page 56); Stonar School (page 58, page 59 bottom).

Every effort has been made to trace and acknowledge copyright holders and anyone else involved in the preparation of this book. However, we apologise in advance for any unintentional omissions.

Contents

Horse and pony points

You've probably heard people using the word 'horse' for both horses and ponies. This is because they are both members of the horse family. However, any horse measuring up to 14.2 **hands** (1.5m/4ft 10in) high at the withers is called a pony. Anything taller is called a horse.

A horse or pony's shape and proportions are called its **conformation**. The parts of the body are called its **points**. It's a good idea to learn these so that you can talk about your pony. Here is Megan the pony showing her points.

The hoof

A horse's foot is called a **hoof**. The outside of the hoof is made of horn. The horn grows all the time, like our fingernails.

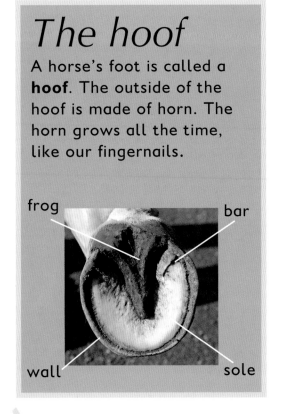

frog
bar
wall
sole

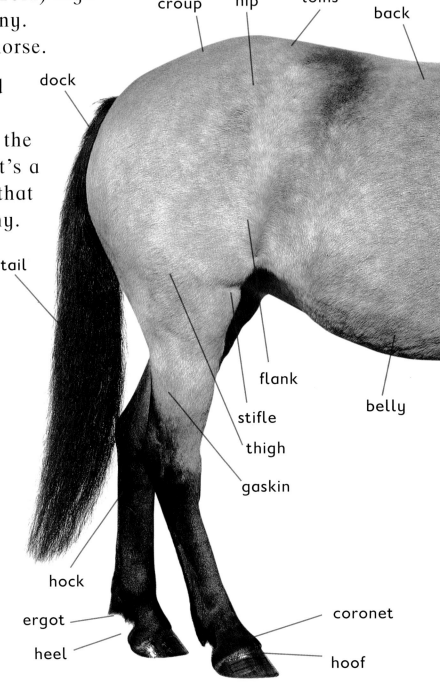

croup
hip
loins
back
dock
tail
flank
belly
stifle
thigh
gaskin
hock
ergot
coronet
heel
hoof

poll

mane

shoulder

crest

withers

forelock

muzzle

cheek

neck

breast

elbow

forearm

knee

cannon

fetlock

pastern

Horse words

Here are some words to describe a horse or pony according to its age and whether it is male or female.

A *foal* is a baby horse up to 1 year old.

A *colt* is a male horse up to 3 years old.

A *dam* is a mother horse.

A *filly* is a female horse up to 3 years old.

A *mare* is a female horse over 4 years old.

A *gelding* is a male horse that has been gelded. This means it cannot breed (make babies).

A *stallion* is a male horse over 3 years old that can breed.

5

Colours and markings

Horses and ponies come in lots of different colours. Some of the colours have names you will recognize, like brown or black, but some are more unusual. It's a good idea to learn the proper names for each of the colours because this is how you describe a horse or pony.

Bay
A bay has a brown body with a black mane, tail and legs.

Brown
A brown pony has a mixture of brown and black hairs covering its body.

Chestnut
A chestnut has an orange-coloured body. The mane and tail are usually a similar colour.

Black
Black ponies have a black coat, mane and tail.

Grey
A pony is called a grey when it is grey or appears white.

Dun
A dun has a sandy-yellow coat, often with a black mane, tail and legs.

Palomino
A palomino has a golden coloured body with an almost white mane and tail.

Skewbald
A skewbald has brown and white patches. A **piebald** has black and white patches.

Roan
A roan is one main colour with a sprinkling of white hairs. Blue roans are black with white. Strawberry roans are chestnut with white.

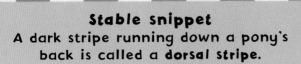

Stable snippet
A dark stripe running down a pony's back is called a **dorsal stripe**.

Markings
Some ponies have white **markings** on their legs or head. Markings are another good way of telling one horse or pony from another.

Face markings

A **star** is a white mark on the forehead.

A **blaze** is a wide white band running down the face.

A **stripe** is a narrow white band running down the face.

A **snip** is a white mark between the nostrils.

Leg markings

A **sock** is a white leg from the hoof to the fetlock joint.

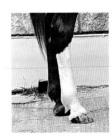

A **stocking** is a white leg that goes up to the knee, or hock.

Common breeds

There are over two hundred types, or **breeds**, of horse and pony in the world. Some breeds, like the Shetland pony, are tiny. Others, such as the Shire horse, are huge. Here are a few of the breeds you might see, or even ride.

Haflinger
The Haflinger, from Austria, is either palomino or chestnut with a flaxen (blonde) mane and tail. Its average height is 14 hands.

Fjord
The Fjord pony, from Norway, has a dun (pale brown) coat and upright mane. It is very tough.

Connemara
The Connemara is from Ireland. It is a good jumper and makes an excellent children's pony. Its average height is 14 hands.

Shire
The Shire is the tallest horse in the world and can grow to over 18 hands. It is usually bay or brown. This Shire has had its tail cut short for work.

Welsh Pony
There are four types of Welsh Pony. The smallest, Section A, is less than 12 hands. The largest is the Welsh Cob which is usually 14 to 15.1 hands. Between these are the Sections B and C.

8

Shetland
The Shetland pony is ideal for small children. Although it is under 10.2 hands, it is very strong.

Hanoverian
The Hanoverian comes from Germany. It is a good showjumping and dressage horse.

Thoroughbred
The thoroughbred is the fastest horse in the world. Most racehorses are thoroughbred.

Arab
The Arab is a beautiful horse, popular throughout the world. It is clever and often frisky.

Lipizzaner
The Lipizzaner comes from Austria. It is famous for being ridden at the Spanish Riding School in Vienna.

The tack

Tack is the name for the things that a horse or pony wears when you ride it. The **saddle** and the **bridle** are the main pieces of tack. These both help you to control the pony and ride safely.

The saddle

The **saddle** goes on the pony's back, then you sit on top of that. The **girth** goes around the pony's belly, to secure the saddle in place. Once on board, you put your feet in the **stirrup** irons. Here, Megan is wearing a general purpose saddle.

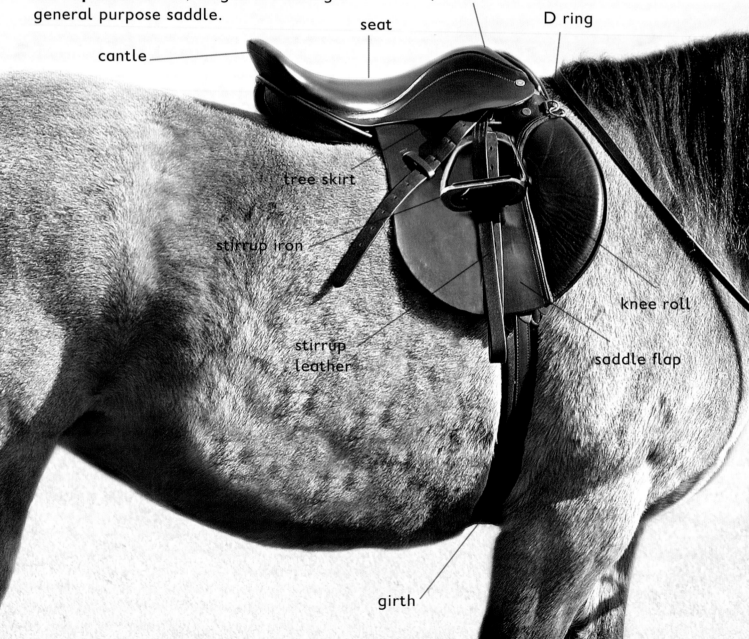

pommel

D ring

seat

cantle

tree skirt

stirrup iron

knee roll

stirrup leather

saddle flap

girth

The bridle and bit

The bridle fits over the pony's head. The bit is the part of the bridle that goes in the pony's mouth. The bit and the bridle help the rider to control the pony. You will probably ride with a **snaffle** bridle like this one. It has a snaffle bit and a single rein.

A **running martingale** is a strap that runs between the girth and the reins. It stops a pony throwing its head too high in the air.

headpiece

browband

A **pelham bit** is stronger than a snaffle. It is useful for strong ponies. This is a rubber pelham.

cheekpiece

noseband

throatlash

snaffle bit

The **double bridle** has two bits and two pairs of reins. It is used by experienced riders for extra control.

reins

Other saddles
There are three main types of saddle: general purpose, **dressage** (right) and jumping.

A **saddle cloth** is put under the saddle to stop it rubbing the pony's back and helps keep the saddle clean.

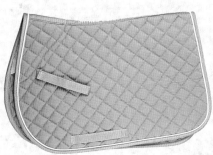

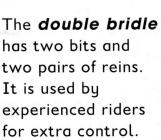

Riding clothes

You will need to wear special clothing to ride safely and comfortably. Although you don't have to wear everything that Elizabeth is wearing in this picture, you should always wear a properly fitted riding hat to protect your head in case you fall off.

Basics

Your **hat** should always be fastened under the chin.

A **body protector** will protect your spine, shoulders and organs if you take a tumble.

Riding gloves have grips on the palms to stop the reins slipping through your fingers.

Jodhpurs are stretchy and make riding more comfortable.

A **crop** or **stick** is used only if your pony ignores your signals. It should never be used in anger.

Jodhpur boots are short and made from leather.

Extras

A **tabard** in a bright fluorescent colour helps you to be seen when riding on the road.

A **sweatshirt** and **hat silk** in your own colours are fun for cross-country.

A waterproof **coat** will keep you dry in wet weather.

Wellington boots are useful for working in the stable or walking in muddy fields.

Riding boots have smooth soles and a heel. They stop your foot sliding through or getting caught in the stirrup.

A **stock** is worn with a collarless shirt.

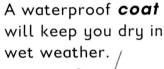

Show jackets are worn for shows or other smart occasions.

Half chaps protect the lower leg from rubbing.

A **tie** looks smart with a shirt and collar.

13

Getting on and off

Getting on and off a horse or pony is called **mounting** and **dismounting**. Here, Anna and her pony Oberon show how it is done.

Mounting

1. Stand beside the pony's shoulder, with the reins and a handful of mane in your left hand. Take the stirrup with your right hand and put your left foot in it.

2. Turn to face the pony's side and catch hold of the saddle with your right hand. Push off the ground with your right leg, until you are standing in the stirrup.

3. Swing your right leg over the pony's back, until you are facing forwards. Push your right foot into the stirrup and hold your reins.

To check your stirrups are the right length, take your feet out of the stirrup irons and let your legs hang down. The base of the iron should be level with your ankle.

Dismounting

1. Take both feet out of your stirrups and put both reins in your left hand.

2. Resting both hands on the front of the saddle, lean forward and swing your right leg over the pony's back.

3. Bring both legs together and, with knees bent, drop to the ground.

Stable snippet
Before mounting, check that the girth is tight enough. You should be able to fit two fingers under the girth. If it's loose, adjust the buckles under the saddle flap.

Your position

The way you sit on a horse or pony is described as your **position**. It's important to have a well balanced position, as it affects the whole riding experience. On this page a dotted line from Jack's heel to his shoulder shows Jack's position on his pony Star.

Sit upright but not too stiffly. You should be able to draw a line through your shoulder and hip, to your heel.

Keep your elbow bent, so that there is a line from it to the horse pony's mouth.

Sit on the lowest part of the saddle. The way you do this is called your **seat**.

Don't grip with your knees. Relax your knees and your thighs.

Look in the direction you are going.

Hold both hands just above the withers. Both hands should be level and a few centimetres apart.

Rest the balls of your feet in the stirrups. Keep your heels slightly down.

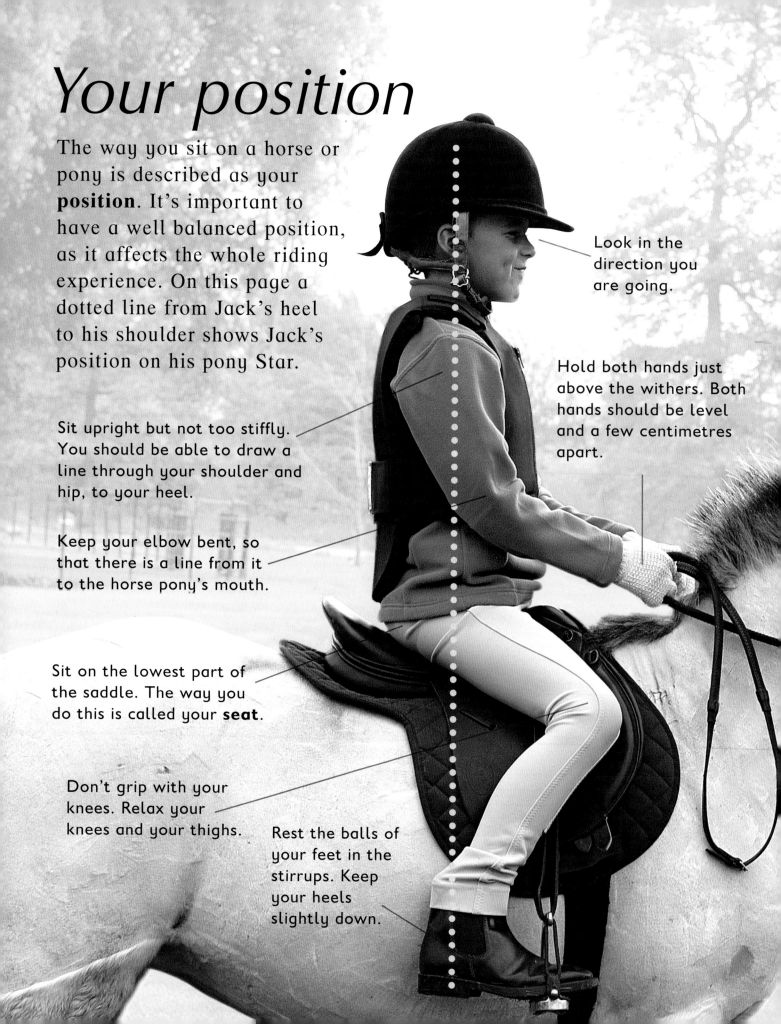

Pass the reins between your little finger and your ring finger, lay them across the next three fingers and pass them out between your index finger and thumb.

The stirrup should be turned outwards so that the leather curves across the inside of your leg.

Stable snippet
Using a **lunge rein** is a great way of improving your position. While the instructor controls the horse with a long rein, you can concentrate on your position.

If Star was magically taken away, Jack should land squarely on his feet with his legs bent.

On the move

As horses and ponies can't talk, you have to let them know what you want by using your legs, hands, body and tone of voice. These are called the **aids**.

Leg aids
Your leg signals tell your pony to turn and move forwards.

Hand aids
Your hand signals guide your pony and make him stop. They are linked to the pony's mouth through the reins and bit. This is called the **contact**. A pony's mouth is soft, so be gentle with your hands. Follow the pony's movement, don't fight against it. Don't pull on the reins. Squeeze them so that it feels like pulling against strong elastic.

Inside or outside?
If your pony is moving to the right, then your inside leg and rein are on the right-hand side and your outside leg and rein are on the left. If your pony is moving to the left, then your inside leg and rein are on the left-hand side and your outside leg and rein are on your right.

Aids for turning
To turn left, look left, and, with your left leg forward, move your right leg behind the girth squeezing with both legs. At the same time, squeeze the left rein and give with your right rein. To turn right, do the opposite.

Voice aids

Your voice can be used to give instructions, such as 'walk' and 'halt'. Here, James is using a soft voice and a pat to tell his pony Pipsqueak that he's a good boy.

The crop

The **crop**, or stick, is an artificial aid. If you squeeze with your legs and the pony ignores you, squeeze again and give the pony a tap with the crop. In the school the crop should usually be carried in the inside hand.

Spurs

Only experienced riders should wear spurs. They are used to back up the leg aids.

Paces

Horses and ponies move at four basic speeds: walk, trot, canter and gallop. These are known as **paces** or **gaits**. On this page, Anna and James put their ponies Oberon and Pipsqueak through their paces.

Walk

James asks his pony Pipsqueak to walk forward by squeezing with both legs. He allows his hands to follow Pipsqueak's head. The movement gently rocks James' hips and stomach.

Trot

Before asking his pony Pipsqueak to trot, James shortens his reins. Then he squeezes with both legs. In a sitting trot he absorbs the movement of the trot. For a rising trot he goes up and down with the rhythm. He pushes into the stirrups and allows his bottom to be lifted out of the saddle on one beat, then gently sits back down on the next. He repeats 'up, down, up, down' in his head.

Canter

Anna asks her pony Oberon to go into a canter from a trot. To do this, Anna stops rising and sits for a few strides. She brushes her outside leg back behind the girth. At the same time she squeezes with her inside leg. She sits well down in the saddle and allows her body to rock with the rhythm of the canter.

Outside leg

Inside leg

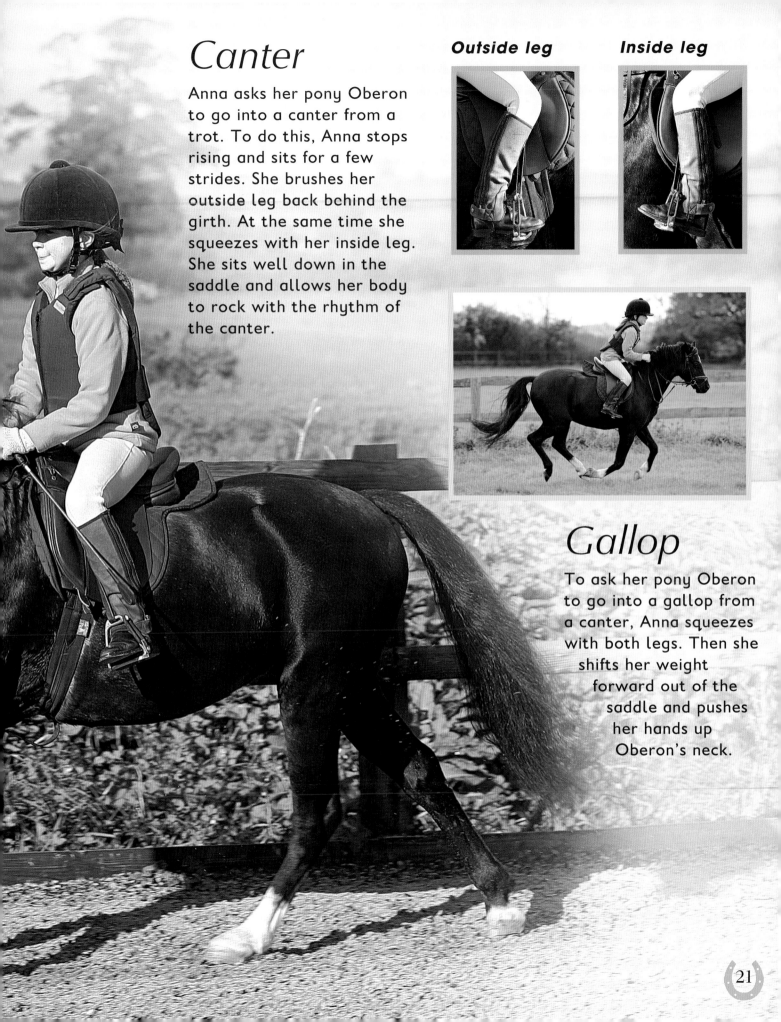

Gallop

To ask her pony Oberon to go into a gallop from a canter, Anna squeezes with both legs. Then she shifts her weight forward out of the saddle and pushes her hands up Oberon's neck.

21

Schooling lessons

Horses and ponies need to learn too. Training a pony is called **schooling**. This is usually done in a flat, fenced rectangular school with a sandy floor. A standard sand school measures 40 metres by 20 metres (131ft by 66ft).

If more than one pony and rider are working in the school, they should pass each other on the left.

Letters are placed around the school, so that you can plan your route, or your instructor can tell you where to go.

C   H   M   E   B   K   F   A

Stable snippet
This saying should help you remember the order the letters appear around the school:
All King Edward's Horses Can Make Big Fences.

Circle

Make a **circle** using half the school. Look in the direction you are going, hold the outside rein firmly and bring the inside rein away from the pony's neck to make it bend slightly. At the same time, nudge with your inside leg (while keeping the outside leg behind the girth). The idea is to make the pony's body follow the curve of the circle.

Figure of eight

A **figure of eight** will help you practise changing your inside leg and rein, and help your pony's flexibility. Practise walking first, then try trotting.

School words

Here are a few schooling terms.
Canter lead – when a pony is cantering around the school it should lead with the inside front leg.
Diagonal – when a pony trots, its legs move in *diagonal* pairs. The diagonal is named after the front leg.
Go large – use the whole school.
Leading file – when you are riding at the front of the group you are leading file.

Changing the rein

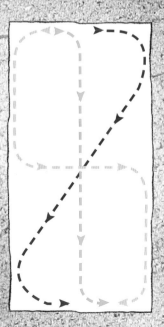

Changing the rein is changing direction. When you are moving to the right you are on the right rein. When you are moving to the left you are on the left rein. To change the rein, cross the school so that you are moving in the opposite direction. Here are some of the ways you can **change the rein** in a school.

Fun exercises

Riding exercises are fun and help you find a better,
safer position. Exercises should be done on a quiet
pony or with someone holding its head.
Elizabeth, Chloe and Jack are doing
exercises on Twinkle, Crunchy
and Star.

Thigh stretch
Quit and cross the stirrups. Hold your ankle and pull your lower leg up towards your bottom. Hold it there for a few seconds, and then do the same on the other side.

Touch your toes
Stretch you right arm up, then bend over and touch your left foot. Do the same thing with your left arm and your right foot.

Twist your body
Hold both arms out to the side, twist to the left, then twist to the right.

Round the world

1. Quit and cross your stirrups. Holding the saddle, swing your left leg over the pony's neck.

2. Swing your right leg over the pony's bottom so that you are facing backwards.

3. Swing your left leg over the pony's bottom. Now swing your right leg to face front.

25

Jumping position

The jumping position is different from the basic riding position. Its aim is to keep you as secure as possible as your pony flies over the jump. Here, Anna shows how it's done on her pony Oberon.

Keep your chin up and look forwards between the pony's ears.

Keep your back flat.

Fold forwards from the hip and slide your bottom backwards.

Your knees should rest against the saddle.

Push more weight into your heels. This will stop you catapulting over the pony's head if it is **refusing** at a jump and stopping suddenly or swerving.

Shorten your stirrups by a hole or two.

Shorten your reins.

You may need to adjust your distances between poles or fences according to the size of your pony, the kind of fence you're jumping and the pony's pace.

Walk around the school in the jumping position. When you feel ready, move on to a trot. Keep this position as you ride over one pole.

Now try three poles 1.2–1.3m (4–4ft 6in) apart. As the pony stretches its neck out over the poles, push your hands forward so that you don't hold him back.

It is important to have a well-balanced jumping position. Here, Anna is practising hers by balancing on a pole.

Starting to jump

Once you are happy with your jumping position, you should be ready to jump a small fence. There are five stages to the jump: approach, take-off, suspension, landing and get-away.

When you and your horse or pony are confident jumping one fence, try two jumps roughly 4.6m (15ft) apart. This measurement will vary depending on the size of your pony and the type of fence.

Slowly build up a small course with different types of fence, such as the crosspole, the upright fence and the spread fence.

1. *Approach*
Sit up straight and line up the pony with the centre of the fence. Look beyond the fence as you approach it. Keep your legs against the pony's sides.

Stable Snippet
Avoid making your pony turn sharply on the approach and get-away.

2. Take-off
As the pony's front feet leave the ground, bend at the hips and push your weight into your heels. Move your hands up towards the pony's ears.

3. Suspension
Look straight ahead as you fly over the fence. This is called 'suspension' because all four feet are suspended off the ground.

4. Landing
As your pony's front feet touch the ground, sit up and look in the direction you want to go. Try not to thump into the saddle.

5. Get-away
Sit up straight, bring your hands back to their normal position without pulling at the reins and turn the pony in the direction you want to go.

Crosspole

Upright

Spread

Riding out

Riding outside the school, or **hacking**, is fun for both you and your horse or pony. When you go hacking for the first time you might want to ask someone to lead you along the road. When you are more experienced, you should be able to ride off the **leading rein**.

On the road

- Always ride with an adult.
- Wear bright reflective clothing so that you can be seen.
- Keep in to the side.
- Look ahead for anything that might frighten your pony.
- Thank drivers who slow down by raising your hand.

Across country

- Keep to bridleways and tracks that horses are allowed on.
- Stay close to the edges of fields.
- Look out for loose barbed wire.
- Shut gates behind you.
- Walk for the last 10 minutes of the ride to allow your pony to cool down.

Opening and closing gates
Teach your pony to stand still while you reach down to open and close a gate.

Handling

Looking after a horse or pony is just as much fun as riding one. However, even the smallest pony can be very strong, so you should always take care that you are **handling** it correctly.

Horse sense

Never creep up behind a horse or pony – you might scare it and make it kick out. Let it know you are coming by saying hello and approaching from the side. Let it sniff your hand and give it a rub on the neck.

Catching your pony

1. Holding the headcollar and leading rein behind your back, walk towards the pony's left-hand side.

2. Standing beside the pony's shoulder, loop the leading rein around its neck and slip the headcollar over its nose.

3. Fasten the headcollar behind the pony's ears.

4. Walk beside the pony's neck as you lead it away.

Quick release knot

Use a quick release knot to tie up a pony. That way, it can be released quickly in an emergency. Tie the rope to a piece of string attached to a metal ring. The string will break if the pony pulls back in fright and prevent it from hurting itself or damaging property.

1. Push the rope through the string and make a loop in the rope.

2. Make another loop in the end of the rope and pull it through the first loop.

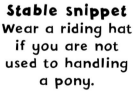

Stable snippet
Wear a riding hat if you are not used to handling a pony.

3. To undo the knot quickly, simply pull on the free end.

Grooming

Horses and ponies need regular cleaning to stay healthy and smart. This is called **grooming**. It is also a good time to get to know your pony. Here Daniel and Sara are grooming their pony Bonny. Sara has to remember to stand to one side as she brushes Bonny's tail.

A **body brush** has fine bristles. It removes natural oils from a pony's coat, so is mainly used for stabled ponies.

1. Start by picking out the hooves. Facing towards the rear end of the pony, run your hand down the pony's leg. Pick up the hoof, then use a hoof pick to clean it out. The sharp point of the hoof pick should point towards the toe. Take care not to dig into the soft frog as you clean out the grooves on either side.

2. Brush the pony's head with a body brush or face brush. Brush the hairs in the direction they grow.

3. Use a dandy brush to remove mud from the pony's body especially where the saddle and bridle will sit.

The **dandy brush** is a stiff brush that removes dried on mud and sweat.

A **water brush** can be used to clean muddy hooves or to dampen down the mane and tail.

A **mane comb** removes tangles from the mane and tail before plaiting.

Keep one **sponge** for the lips, eyes and nostrils. Use another one for under the tail.

A **sweat scraper** removes sweat or water after you've washed a pony down.

A **metal curry comb** removes the dirt from a body brush.

A **plastic curry comb** removes stubborn mud. Don't use it on sensitive parts of the body.

4. Pick out hay and tangles from the mane and tail with your fingers. Then brush one section at a time with a body brush.

A **hoof pick** removes mud and stones from the feet.

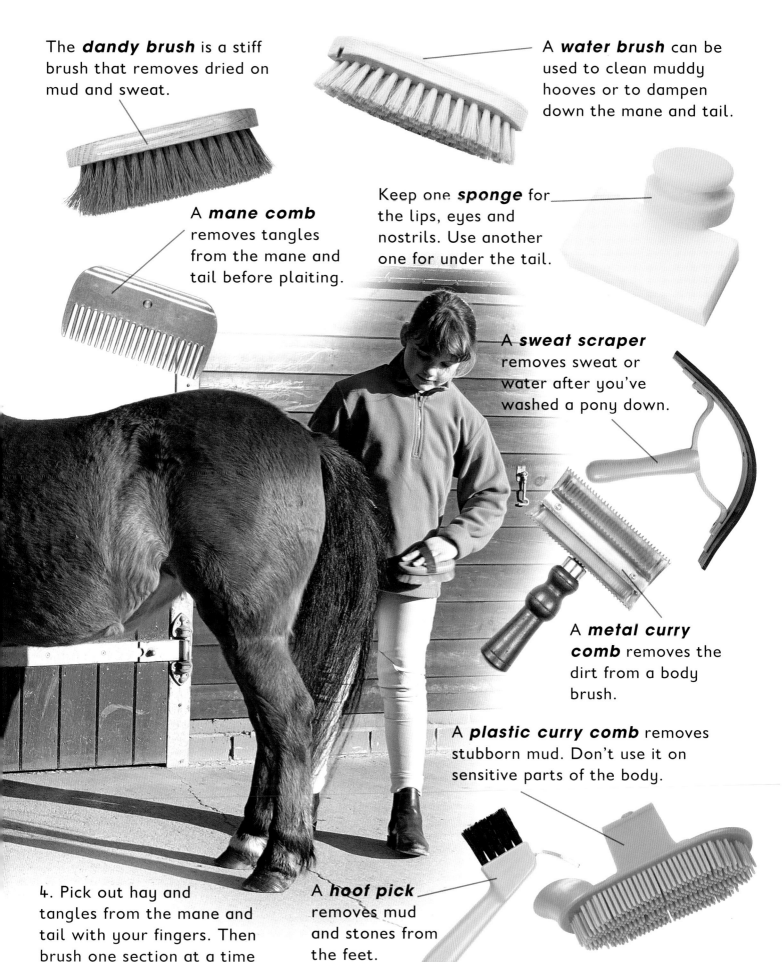

35

Tacking up

Putting the tack on a horse or pony is called **tacking up**. It is a good idea to watch an experienced person tack up before you try yourself.

Putting on the saddle

Elizabeth shows us how to put the saddle on her pony Twinkle.

1. Hold the saddle on your left arm with the pommel near the crook of your elbow.

2. Approach the pony on its left (near) side. Lift the saddle onto the pony's back, just in front of the withers. Slide it back into position.

3. Go to the other side of the saddle and let the girth down. Return to the near side and pull the end of the girth under the pony's tummy. Buckle the girth to the straps under the saddle flap.

Here Chloe is leading Twinkle all ready and tacked up.

Putting on the bridle

Now Jack shows us how to put on Twinkle's bridle.

1. Stand on the pony's left side. Put the reins over the pony's neck. Then take off the headcollar.

2. Holding the top of the bridle in your right hand, slip it over the pony's nose. Open its mouth by pressing your thumb in the corner of the mouth.

3. Slide the bit into its mouth and lift the top of the bridle over its ears.

4. Do up the throatlash and fasten the noseband. Tuck any loose straps into their loops (keepers).

Stable Snippet
To take off the bridle, undo the throatlash and noseband, then gently lift the bridle over the pony's ears. Put your hand under the bit as you slide it out of the pony's mouth so that it doesn't bash against its teeth.

Cleaning tack

Cleaning tack might not seem like much fun but it's a very important job. It helps the tack to last longer and gets rid of any nasty bits of dirt that might otherwise rub against the horse or pony. Sara and Daniel are cleaning Bonny's bridle and saddle.

Cleaning the bridle

1. Hang the bridle on a bridle hook, with the throatlash and noseband unbuckled.

2. Use lukewarm water and a sponge to clean any dirt from the bit and all the leather parts of the bridle. Then dry the leather with a soft cloth.

3. Rub saddle soap onto all the leather bits, using a slightly damp sponge.

Cleaning the saddle

1. Put the saddle on a saddle horse. Unbuckle the girth, stirrup leathers and irons. Soak non-leather girths.

2. Use lukewarm water and a sponge to clean the saddle, stirrup leathers and leather girths. Dry the leather with a soft cloth.

3. Rub saddle soap all over the saddle and stirrup leathers using a damp sponge.

4. Clean the stirrup irons in warm water then polish with a soft cloth.

Stable snippet
Bridles should be taken apart at least once a month, so that they can be checked for wear and thoroughly cleaned.

Horse clothes

As well as tack for riding, your horse or pony might wear other things to help keep it warm, protected and safe when you are not riding. Nell is wearing some of the basics.

A **headcollar** fits around the pony's head.

A **leading rein** is attached to the headcollar to lead or tie up a pony.

This **cooler** helps keep the pony warm and dry after exercise or being washed down.

Leg bandages keep the pony's legs warm and protect them when travelling in a horsebox.

Rugs

A **turnout rug** keeps the pony warm and dry outside during the winter months, especially if your pony has had its winter coat **clipped**.

A **stable rug** is a thick rug worn in the stable.

Boots

Boots protect a pony's legs from injury when it is being ridden or travelling in a horsebox.

A **tail bandage** protects the pony's tail while travelling. It also flattens the hairs at the top of the tail.

Brushing boots stop a pony from hurting itself if it hits one leg against the other.

Over-reach boots go over the front hooves. They stop a pony from hurting its heels if it knocks them with its back feet.

Tendon boots protect the pony's front legs, especially while jumping. They are open at the front so that the pony can feel if it knocks a pole down.

Travelling boots protect the pony's legs when it is travelling.

Feeding

What you feed your horse or pony depends on the time of year, how much work it is doing, and whether you keep it in or out.

These two horses, Daisy and Yally, are happy eating grass. But if the grass is poor, they will need to be fed extra hay.

Ponies need clean drinking water.

Stable snippet
When feeding from your hand, hold your palm flat with your thumbs tucked out of the way.

42

A pony that lives in a stable will need to be fed hay at least three times a day.

Food for energy

Feeding a pony special pony cubes, or other hard feeds, will give it extra energy if you ride it a lot.

There are lots of different feeds. Ask an expert what you should feed your pony.

Hay is dried grass. Horses and ponies should only be fed good quality hay.

Chaff or **chop** is either chopped hay or chopped hay and straw. It can be added to pony nuts to help digestion.

Oats make some horses and ponies excitable, so should not be fed to children's ponies.

Coarsemix is a mixture of cereal and pellets with added vitamins and minerals.

Nuts or **cubes** are pellets of dried food.

Ponies love **carrots** and **apples**. Cut them lengthways, as chunks can make a pony choke.

In the stable

There should be
somewhere to
tie a haynet.

Most ponies prefer to live out all or
part of the time. But sometimes,
particularly during a cold winter, you
may need to bring them inside. If they
are stabled all the time, make sure
that they have plenty of exercise and
are fed regularly.

The stable or stall

The ideal pony stable is at least 3.6m
by 3m (12ft by 10ft), big enough for a
pony to walk around and lie down in.
A horse's stable should be at least
3.6m square (12ft square).

Mucking out

A stable needs to be cleaned out at least
once a day. Elizabeth and Sara are
mucking out Popcorn's stable.
Remove any droppings and wet
bedding. Push the remaining
bedding against the walls and
sweep the floor clean.

Your pony will need
clean drinking water
at all times.

44

A window provides fresh air and somewhere for a pony to look out.

Livery

If you have nowhere to keep a pony, or can't look after it yourself, you can pay a stable yard. This is called keeping your pony at **livery**. Full livery is when everything is done for you. All you do is turn up and ride. Part livery is when you spend some of the time looking after your pony. DIY livery is when the yard provides the field and stable, and you do the rest yourself.

Stable snippet
If you have to muck out while your pony is in the stable, tie it up first.

Bedding down
Once the floor has dried, put the old bedding back down and add new bedding.

Straw, wood shavings and shredded paper all make good bedding.

In the field

Horses and ponies love being **turned out** in a field with other horses or ponies. Make sure that the field is safe and that there is water and shelter. They don't need much grooming because the natural oil in their coats keeps them warm and dry. But check them for cuts or other injuries at least once a day. Pick out their feet and make sure their rugs are fastened.

Most ponies can live out all year round without a rug. But horses, and some clipped ponies, will be happier in a waterproof turnout rug during the colder months.

A field shelter protects your pony from the wind and rain in the winter, and from the burning sun and insects in the summer. If you don't have a field shelter, hedges or trees can provide shelter.

Gates should be secure and wide enough for a pony to walk through easily.

Check that water is available at all times. You may need to break ice in winter.

Fencing should be strong. Wooden railing is best. Never use barbed wire, as a pony can get tangled up in it and hurt itself.

Poisonous plants

Check the field for any poisonous plants. If you find any, get an adult to spray them or pull them out.

Ragwort   **Acorns**   **Yew**   **Bracken**

Also look out for deadly nightshade, foxgloves and privet.

47

Preparing for a show

Riding at home or in a riding school is great fun, but there's nothing quite like a show to test your riding skills. Part of the fun is making sure both you and your pony look as smart as possible.

Get as much as possible ready the night before.

Clean your tack. Wash your saddle cloth and girth.

Polish your jodhpur boots and brush your jacket and hat. Make sure you have a clean shirt and jodhpurs.

If your pony has white socks or a light mane and tail wash them in shampoo and rinse thoroughly. You should also sponge any grass stains.

Brush your pony until its coat gleams.

If you want to look extra smart, plait the pony's mane and tail.

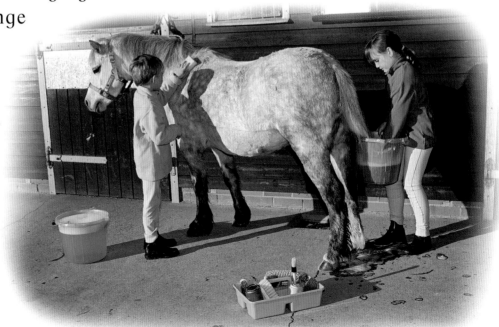

Plaiting the mane

1. Dampen the mane and divide it into equal sections. Start behind the ear and plait each section. Fasten each plait with a rubber band.

2. Roll each plait up and loop the band around the plait.

3. Don't forget the forelock.

Plaiting the tail

1. Dampen the tail. Then take three sections from the top of the tail and start plaiting.

2. Plait down the centre. Add sections from each side as you work your way down.

3. Three-quarters of the way down the dock, stop adding the side hairs and plait down the centre. At the end, loop it under and secure with a band.

Shoeing and foot care

Although ponies' feet are made from tough horn, they are designed for roaming free in the wild, not for riding along roads with a passenger on their back. So most ponies have metal shoes nailed to their feet. This is called **shoeing**. Pick out your pony's feet daily. Check that the shoes aren't loose and that there's no serious cracking.

A pony will need new shoes every four to eight weeks.

Stable Snippet
Never ride a pony if it loses a shoe, as it will make it unbalanced and make its foot sore.

The **farrier**, Mike Roberts, is shoeing Boots. He will remove the old shoes, trim the horse's feet, make sure that the new shoes fit properly, and nail them in place. Don't worry, the nails won't hurt Boots.

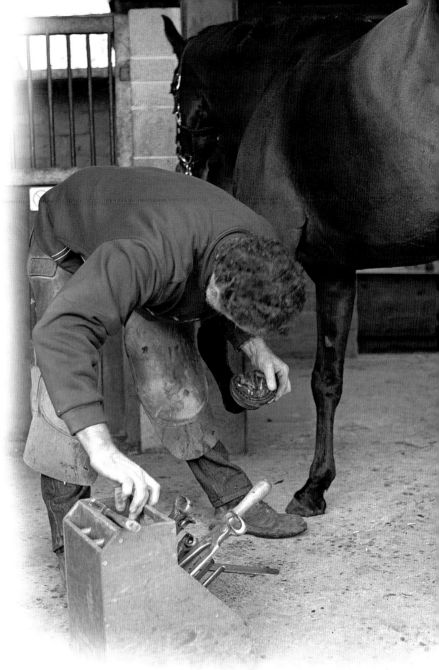

The farrier makes sure that the shoe fits while it is still hot. If it needs any small changes, he puts it on an anvil and hammers it into shape.

Hooves grow all the time so, even if your pony is not being ridden, it will need its feet trimmed regularly by the farrier.

51

Common problems

Like all animals, horses and ponies get sick from time to time. It's a good idea to learn to recognize some of the most common problems. Then you can ask an expert for advice and, if necessary, call out a vet.

Lameness

When a horse or pony limps, it is said to be lame. Lameness can be caused by a lot of things. First of all check that it doesn't have a stone in its foot. Then look for any obvious cuts or swellings. If the pony is very lame, you should call a vet. Never ride a lame horse or pony.

Laminitis

Laminitis is a painful swelling in the foot. Ponies get it from eating too much rich grass or not getting enough exercise. Pony's with laminitis will often lean back on their heels and be unwilling to walk. The hooves will feel warm. Call your vet if you think your pony has laminitis.

Mud fever

If you see scabs on your pony's legs, it could be mud fever. Mud fever is an infection caused by muddy or very dusty conditions. Antibiotic cream should clear it up.

Colic

Colic is a painful belly ache. The horse or pony becomes distressed and often breaks into a sweat. It may start stamping its feet and looking round at its belly. As the pain gets worse, it may want to lie down and roll. If you suspect colic, you should call the vet at once.

Strangles

This is a throat infection. The horse or pony will have a swelling around its throat, a high temperature and a runny nose. Strangles can be passed on easily so, if you think your pony might have it, keep it away from other ponies and call a vet.

Wounds

If you find a small wound on your pony, wash it with clean water and apply antibiotic spray or powder. If you find a larger wound, call a vet.

Strange behaviour

Biting is a bad habit. If your pony bites you, say 'no' firmly.

Bolting is when a pony runs away with you. If this happens, turn the pony in a tight circle.

Bucking is when a pony kicks its back legs into the air with its back arched. If your pony bucks regularly, get its back and tack checked by an expert.

Napping is when a pony refuses to go forward. If this happens, squeeze with both legs and, if it still won't move, use a stick.

Shying is when a pony jumps because it is frightened. This is not bad behaviour and should not be punished.

Rearing is when a pony lifts both front legs off the ground. If your pony rears, lean forward and don't pull on the reins.

Horsing around

By now you will have discovered just how much fun riding or owning a horse or pony can be. But it doesn't have to end there. Look in any local paper, or pony magazine, and you will find a whole range of activities that you and your pony can take part in. Try out a few and see which ones suit you best.

Pony racing
Pony racing is becoming increasingly popular.

Pony clubs
Most areas have a local pony club. The club will arrange camps and rallies where instructors will teach small groups everything from pony care to jumping and dressage. Pony clubs also organize fun rides, demonstrations and competitions.

Gymkhanas

Gymkhanas are fun competitions for young riders. They are made up of different mounted games, including egg and spoon, relay and beanbag races. Silk **rosettes** are given to the first six ponies and riders to cross the line.

Fun rides

Fun rides are organized rides through the countryside for both adults and children. There are often optional jumps. They are not races. Riders don't all start at the same time and can take as long as they want. If you and your horse enjoy fun rides, you might want to move on to **endurance** riding. This is long-distance riding, usually over 80km (50 miles) long.

In the ring

You will need a well-behaved and well-schooled pony to enter dressage or showing competitions. You must wear the correct smart clothing and your pony must be beautifully turned out. In the dressage arena your horse or pony is given points during a test which includes certain movements. In the showring your pony is judged on it's conformation, paces and behaviour. There are competitions for all levels so you can compete against riders of a similar ability.

Dressage
During a dressage test points out of ten are given for walking, trotting, cantering and halting at certain markers to see how well your pony is trained.

Showing

There are many different classes to choose from, including show pony, riding pony, show hunter pony, working hunter pony, and mountain and moorland. There are also in-hand classes, where a pony is led, and leading rein classes for younger riders. It is important to enter the right class for your type of pony. In ridden classes you will ride around the ring with the other competitors, then be asked to perform your own individual show. This should include walk, trot and canter on both reins.

Jumping competitions

If you enjoy jumping, there are lots of different competitions to look out for.

Show jumping

Show jumping is a competition in which you jump a course of fences. There are classes for all abilities. The classes are organized by the height of the fences, your age and the height of the pony. There are even leading rein classes. You get **faults** if you knock down a fence, fall off or if your pony refuses a jump. If you jump the course in the wrong order you are disqualified. A **clear round** is one with no mistakes. If there are lots of clear rounds, there will be a timed **jump off.**

Hunter trials

In hunter trials you jump a course of cross-country fences (rustic fences that don't fall down when knocked) within a set time. Riders are not told the time until the end of the competition. The winner is the horse and rider who jumped a clear round nearest to the given time.

Horse trials

Horse trials, also known as **events**, last for one, two or three days. There are at least three parts: show jumping, dressage and cross-country. To do well you need a horse or pony which is good at everything.

Western riding

Western riding is an American cowboy style. It is perfect for working the large ranches in America. The long stirrups mean that the rider can sit comfortably at all paces. Holding the reins in one hand means that the other hand is free for roping cattle.

Western bridles don't have a nose band. Some have bits and some don't.

The Western saddle looks very different from other saddles. Like the bridles, they are often highly decorated.

Western horses are very quick on their feet and respond to the slightest movement of the rein against their neck.

Glossary

Aids   The actions a rider uses to tell a horse or pony what to do.

Bay   A brown horse or pony with dark mane, tail and legs.

Bedding down   Preparing new bedding after mucking out.

Bit   The metal part of the bridle that fits in the horse or pony's mouth.

Black   A black horse or pony with black mane, tail and legs.

Blaze   A wide white marking running in a band down the horse or pony's face.

Body protector   A strengthened jacket that protects the rider's upper body.

Bolting   A horse or pony racing off out of control.

Breed   A variety of horse or pony that has particular characteristics.

Bridle   The leather harness that fits over the horse or pony's head.

Bridleway   A special footpath that horses and riders can use.

Brown   A horse or pony which is almost black with brown points.

Bucking   A horse or pony jumping into the air with its back arched and hind legs stretched out.

Chaps   Leather leggings worn to protect the rider's legs.

Chestnut   A horse or pony with an orange-coloured coat, mane and tail.

Circle   A schooling exercise where the pony is ridden in a small or large circle.

Clip   The shaved area of a horse or pony's winter coat to stop them sweating too much and losing weight when they're exercised.

Colt   A male horse or pony up to 3 years old.

Conformation   The shape and proportions of a horse or pony.

Contact   The connection through the reins between the rider's hands and the horse or pony's mouth.

Crop   A stick used to back up your leg aids.

Dam   A foal's mother.

Diagonal   The opposite pair of front and back legs that the horse or pony moves during a trot.

Dismounting   Getting off a horse or pony.

Dock   The fleshy part at the top of the horse or pony's tail from which the hairs grow.

Dorsal stripe   A dark line running down the back of a horse or pony.

Dressage   A competition where the horse or pony is judged on the way it performs certain movements.

Dun   A sandy coloured horse or pony often with a black mane, tail and legs.

Endurance riding   A long-distance ride which can be up to 80km (50 miles).

Event   A competition that includes jumping, dressage and cross-country riding.

Farrier   A person trained to shoe and trim a horse or pony's hooves.

Faults   Penalty points for falling off, knocking down or refusing a fence.

Figure of eight   A schooling exercise where the pony is ridden in a figure of eight.

Filly   A female horse or pony up to 3 years old.

Foal   A baby horse or pony up to 1 year old.

Forelegs   The front legs.

Gait   Another word for pace. They are walk, trot, canter, gallop.

Gelding   1. A male horse or pony that has been gelded. 2. A male horse or pony that is not able to breed.

Girth   The strap that goes around the horse or pony's belly to hold the saddle in place.

Grey   A horse or pony that is grey or looks almost white.

Grooming   To brush and clean a horse or pony.

Gymkhana   A fun competition that includes games and races.

Hacking   Riding outside the school.

Hand   The unit used to measure the height of a horse or pony. One hand is equal to 10cm (4 in).

Handling   The way you behave around horses.

Inside leg   The rider's leg that is on the same side as the direction the pony is moving in.

Inside rein   The rein that is on the same side as the direction the pony is moving in.

Jodhpurs   Riding trousers with strengthened patches on the inside leg.

Jump off   A timed section of a show jumping competition where there is no clear winner.

Leading rein   1. A rope used to lead a pony.

2. A rider is said to be on a leading rein when he or she is being led.

Livery stable A place where people can pay to stable their horses or ponies.

Lunge rein A long rein attached to the horse or pony's head that allows someone on the ground to control it with a whip and their voice.

Mare A female horse or pony over 4 years old.

Markings The white shapes on a horse or pony's head and legs that help identify it.

Martingale A long strap used to stop a pony throwing its head too high in the air.

Mounting Getting on a horse or pony.

Mucking out Cleaning out a stable.

Napping Refusing to go forward.

Nearside The left-hand side of a horse or pony.

Offside The right-hand side of a horse or pony.

Outside leg The rider's leg that is on the opposite side to the direction the pony is moving in.

Outside rein The rein that is on the opposite side to the direction the pony is moving in.

Pace A walk, trot, canter or gallop. Each pace has its own rhythm as the horse or pony's feet touch the ground. A walk has a four-time rhythm, a trot has a two-time rhythm, a canter has a three-time rythm and a gallop has a four-time rhythm.

Palomino A golden coloured horse or pony often with blonde mane, tail and legs.

Piebald A horse or pony with black and white patches.

Points 1. The parts of a horse or pony. 2. The mane, tail, muzzle, tips of the ears and lower legs.

Position The way a rider sits in the saddle.

Rearing A horse or pony rising up on its back legs.

Refusing A horse or pony stopping in front of a jump.

Roan A horse or pony with one main colour and a sprinkling of white hairs.

Rosettes Ribbons shaped like roses, given as prizes at events.

Saddle A shaped leather seat that fastens around the horse or pony's back.

Schooling Training a horse or pony to improve its obedience and flexibility.

Seat 1. The way a rider sits in the saddle. 2. The part of the saddle that the rider sits on.

Shoeing Attaching metal shoes to the horse or pony's hoof usually done by the farrier.

Showing A competition where a horse or pony is judged on its conformation, paces and behaviour.

Shying A horse or pony jumping sideways usually when it is frightened.

Skewbald A horse or pony with brown and white patches.

Snip A white marking between the horse or pony's nostrils.

Sock A white marking on the horse or pony's leg from its hoof to its fetlock.

Star A white marking on the horse or pony's forehead.

Stirrup The metal part of a saddle where a rider puts their feet.

Stallion A male horse or pony over 3 years old that has not been gelded

Stock A rider's neckscarf worn for smart occasions.

Stocking A white marking on the horse or pony's leg from its hoof to its knee or hock.

Stripe A narrow white marking running in a band down the horse or pony's face.

Tack The bridle and saddle.

Tacking up Putting on the bridle and saddle

Turn out 1. To put a horse or pony in a field. 2. The way a pony and rider look for competition.

Index